MW00679176

Wonderful Wednesdays

FIFTY-TWO CONVERSATIONS FOR COUPLES

Eddie and Sylvia Robertson

Wonderful Wednesdays

Published by Yawn's Publishing
210 East Main Street
Canton, GA 30114
www.yawnsbooks.com

Library of Congress Control Number: 2012939585

ISBN: 978-1-936815-51-7
978-1-938615-53-1 e-book

Printed in the United States

Prologue

Every couple we know needs more time to talk together than the busyness of life easily allows. There is always another necessity, another demand, competing for our time and energy. Yet, we know that keeping in regular touch with each other helps our marriage to survive and to thrive. We believe the practice will prove valuable for you as well.

Gifted with ***Better Marriages*** since 1976, we have been privileged to listen to couples sharing aloud the triumphs and trials of their marriage journeys. Their authenticity has touched our hearts and encouraged us to deal with similar issues and happenings in our lives. They have helped us to grow. After forty three years, we are still growing.

This book is our attempt to pass along to you some of the love given to us. Presented for you are fifty two dialogue opportunities for the weeks of the year through the four seasons. The anecdotes and thoughts shared are personal; yet, this book is not about us. The entries offer opportunities to explore and grow in your own marriage relationship. They focus on communication, creative use of inevitable conflict, and commitment to growth in marriage. The skills used build upon each other through the year. The title ***Wonderful Wednesdays*** originated with intentional weekly events planned for just the two of us. ***Knee to knee*** is marriage enrichment speak for spouses turning face to face, taking hands, and giving each other undivided attention.

Ideally, we ask you to set aside regular weekly time to talk together. We do know, however, that life is complicated. We hope you will use these suggestions for dialogue whenever you can. We wish you blessings as you get to know each other better and stay in touch—*knee to knee*, hand in hand, and heart to heart.

Eddie and Sylvia Robertson
2012

Winter

Is There Hope for Marriage?

Is there hope for marriage today? We believe there is hope, but, as with all valuable things, marriages must be protected and nurtured. Our son, Nate, trail named Maple Leaf, hiked the Appalachian Trail, Georgia to Maine, in 1996. Day hikers and Scouts repeatedly asked two questions: "Have you seen any bears?" and "What do you eat?" He answered, "Yes, there are bears, and they will steal your food. You have to hang your pack up high and always assume there are bears around." The second answer was "Peanut Butter and Mac and Cheese."

In our life as a couple, there are many "bears" which will steal time and joy from our relationship. They don't respect what is in our "pack;" we have to keep it out of their reach. Likewise, the essential "food" of our relationship is talking with and listening to each other, building a life in tandem. We must stay up to date with each other. We do this by setting aside at least a little time often to look at each other and share our lives.

Think about the following questions. Take time to turn to your mate and share your thoughts. Listen to your mate's thoughts *knee to knee.*

What do you appreciate about your marriage?

Who or what are your "bears?" They might even be people and things you like.

How do you secure your marriage "pack?"

What "food" sustains you and your marriage for the long haul?

How can you get and keep more of that "good food?"

Little Things Mean a Lot

When we were children, we went to Kresge's or the Ben Franklin. We called them "dime stores;" today, we go to some rendition of a "Dollar Store." These emporiums are full of little things; some are necessities, and some are just doodads that make life nicer. We listed things we have bought at a "Dollar Store": detergent and cleaning supplies, a light for a Christmas nativity scene, stocking stuffers and holiday pot holders, Teddy Bears for Sweetheart Breakfast centerpieces, puzzles for visiting children, patio lights and candles.

In marriages, little things can mean a lot. They can be words like "thank you," "excuse me," "I'm sorry," or "Hubba Hubba." They can be calls to say "How is your day going?" or a "phone photo," an unexpected flower, taking the garbage out, helping clean cat boxes, bringing coffee or a cold drink, or laying out vitamins.

These little things may only take a minute, but they are not just niceties; they are necessities that reaffirm daily that we are happy to be married to each other. Little things strengthen the bond between us.

In what little ways do you show your appreciation for your mate with words or actions?

In what ways do you hear or see your mate showing appreciation for you?

Make some lists and share them with your mate *knee to knee*.

Building a Team

Watching the phoebes building nests around our porch reminds us of the early days of our marriage when we were making our first home, our first nest, together. We undertook the task of wallpapering our kitchen in a tiny old house. We had different standards, and we both thought we were "right." Giving up being "right" was difficult. It meant having to work as a team instead of competing. It meant giving up having the last word. It meant recognizing that Ed's gift was dunking the long sheets of paper in the claw footed bathtub, dragging them to the kitchen, and holding the weight while Sylvia climbed the ladder and matched the pattern. Even then, the job was not perfect; the paper was railroad salvage, the paste was old, the walls were slick with years of bright yellow enamel paint. Ultimately, yellow stripes bloomed between the panels.

Years later, we still laugh about the wallpaper job, but we learned lessons. We learned that being "right" as individuals felt good for a little while but did not get us where we wanted to go as a couple. We learned that we were a team of imperfect humans. We learned to recognize and honor each other's gifts.

In life, there is always some slippage between the neatly matched patterns. When the edges pull apart, we have learned to intentionally stop the action and start over again as a team.

What complementary gifts and skills do you and your mate have?

Does always being "right" get you where you want to go as a couple?

How do you tell each other when you want to stop the action and start over so that you can better match your behavior to the goal of building your marital team?

Think about these questions and share your responses with your mate *knee to knee.*

Words are Important!

Couples marry with the best of intentions. We seek the shared privacy of that intimate relationship. We revel in the delight of it. We think we can weather anything, as long as we are together. The luckiest people are those who are married to their best friends. Unfortunately, like the best friends of childhood, we can grow to take our mates for granted. We have busy lives, and we assume our mates know they are loved. It is said that actions speak louder than words, but actions have to be interpreted. Sometimes mates need to hear the words.

Words are important! Everybody knows words can hurt, but words can also affirm and heal. The child in each of us needs to hear that we are loved and deemed worthy of being loved: "I love your presence beside me through good times and bad." "It fills my heart when I tap on the window and you look up and smile." "You are my favorite playmate." You are the Best!" "I love your laugh." "You make pretty babies!"

Think of five affirmations for your mate.

I love you when…

I appreciate…

I enjoy…

You don't have to wait for an anniversary or Valentine's Day. Take time to look at each other and share words of love *knee to knee*.

Intentional Romance

On the day after Christmas, the stores fill with everything imaginable in red, pink, and chocolate in anticipation of Valentine's Day. Husbands are terror stricken as they try to choose a Valentine. Will it be romantic enough? Wives wonder if "he" will remember and worry about how to tell their husbands they are loved.

If romance is magical, but does not happen by magic, how do we get it? We all know that romance can get lost in reality. If we want to keep some of that wonderful magic, we have to choose to do so. In choosing intentional romance, we express more love than if romance did happen magically. Romance bonds us in marriage and deserves special attention and a place in our budget. Romance places our focus on our mate, whom we can affirm and cherish like no one else. Regular doses of romance can be tucked into ordinary days. How about monthly anniversary dates, "remembering when" on the swing, volunteering to call the sitter, or sightseeing close to home? Romance is only as far away as your shared imaginations!

Talk about it *knee to knee.*

What view of romance did you learn when you were growing up?

What expectations did you bring to marriage about romance? Have you shared those wishes with your mate?

What would you find romantic?

How could you best say "I love you" this Valentine's Day or any day?

Freefall versus Intentionality

Living without structure, responsibilities, or plans may seem attractive when we are feeling weighed down by cares, but marriages do not do well in freefall. Too much of value is left to chance. Our baby marriage needed a map. We had hopes and dreams but few instructions. We were fortunate to be invited to an early *Better Marriages* group. We were given the gift of intentionality. We learned to deliberately make plans and were taught the skills to listen, to speak, and to use information from conflict to grow our marriage. We are still supported today as we shape our marriage map.

What expectations and dreams do you have?

What plans do you have?

What skills do you have or need?

Where can you be supported?

Share *knee to knee*

Snow Days

It has snowed for three days. We are snowed in at the bottom of the hill; no car is going back up for a day or two. The land line is out, and there is no cell signal. The television reception is lousy. We are grateful for dry firewood, for a supply of food, and for electricity (for now). What shall we do?

We have the opportunity to sit and look at each other. We have time to talk and listen. We have time to watch the birds come to the feeders in crowds, to read aloud to each other. We have time to venture into the chilly white, to watch our warm breath in the cold air, to sled downhill on salvaged cardboard, to pelt each other with snowballs, to giggle and squeal, to race for the house, to stamp snow from our boots and toss wet coats where we won't step in their puddles. We have time to make popcorn and hold hot tea cups in our cold hands. We have time for other couple pastimes and to cuddle and to nap.

Use your imagination—what would you want to do if you and your spouse were "snowed in?"

How can you make your own "Snow Day?" You don't even need any real snow—just some set aside, prioritized, private time.

Spend some time brainstorming with your mate *knee to knee.* You may not be able to really control the weather, but you can plan some time for each other.

Contagion

Do you ever feel alone as a couple? Many people may have wished you well when you married. Even so, daily life is busy for them, and they may not think to lift you up regularly. Meanwhile, marriage saboteurs are everywhere. Comics, gossips, lovers of drama, and avoiders of their own problems are ready and waiting to tear at the fabric of marriages. Co-workers and so-called friends are often full of advice about "looking out for number one." They may encourage you to justify any negative feelings rather than to examine them. They seldom ask what you want for your marriage and support you as you think through your own behaviors, even those you might choose to change. Work places teem with people full of bitterness who want to share. Anti-marriage talk is contagious. Beware.

Couples can deliberately limit contact with anti-marriage environments and seek out helpful friends and groups who are happy to be supportive in hard times and to rejoice in joyful times.

Consider the people who surround you *knee to knee.*

Are they supportive of you as an individual and of you and your spouse as a couple?

Who encourages you?

When times are rough, who shows you and your spouse that you are not alone?

With whom can you share your delight in your marriage?

Do you need to consider some changes in the company you keep?

Being with You

Love is being with you as you came down the aisle on your Daddy's arm.

Love is being with you when Charity and Nathan were born.

Love is being with you at graduations and weddings.

Love is being with you missing our dads.

Love is holding your hand as we watch Emily have her kittens.

Love is holding your hand as the drip of the chemo enters your vein.

Love is sitting beside you in hospital rooms.

Love is feeding Mom avocado and crackers.

Love is being with you on the journey.

What is love?

Love is being with you when…

Share *knee to knee*

Multi-Tasking is Over-Rated

In today's culture, multi-tasking (as driving, talking, eating, and working all at the same time) is seen as valuable. Pastors, teachers, and theaters see the need to admonish us to turn our phones "to silent operation." Fixing dinner, watching TV, and tending kids happens all at once.

It is rare for our full attention to go to any one thing, including our mates. In spite of everything to be done, husbands and wives deserve each other's full attention in prime time; Couples need to talk, listen, check in, and keep their ships going in the same direction. We need to say, "I need you to listen to me." It is okay to "put the kids (or cats) on mute," to keep bed times, to turn off the TV. It is good to make dates with each other in INK on the calendar, to say "no" to some requests from others. It is important to make and keep couple time. Couples need to connect daily, even if only for short periods of time.

What interferes with having prime time together?

How can you connect with each other more often and in more satisfying ways?

Make a plan *knee to knee.*

Something Different

Spending a leisurely few days at the lake in Michigan, we enjoyed watching the variety of birds swooping into the snow covered feeders. We noticed that the sparrows had distinct spots on their gray vests, different from the streaks of the chipping sparrows we expected to see. With that recognition of difference, we consulted the bird guide and discovered that we were being visited by American Tree Sparrows, winter migrants from the sub-arctic. The next morning in the sunshine, we also recognized that their beaks were yellow and black.

Putting a name on anything allows us to look for finer detail. This is true in nature and in marriage. Sharing awareness of things that are different keeps married people in touch with each other. When he says, "I see (or I feel or I think) something different," he is giving information about himself. She honors his sharing about himself, when she responds, "I hear you see something different; Can you tell me more?" There is an opportunity for growth in their marriage.

Differences can be about many things: "I think I may want to sing in the choir." "I notice that I seem to get depressed around this time of year." "I am feeling proud of you." "I really enjoyed our walk the other day, and I would like to walk with you more often." "I think I hear a happier tone in your voice lately."

Share some time with your spouse *knee to knee*.

Ask each other: "Are you aware of anything new or different lately?" Listen openly.

Respond to each other: "Tell me more."

Acting on the Pinch

When the chemical charge of infatuation dissipates, couples become two imperfect humans sharing the same space. Nerves are exposed. It is inevitable that what was sometimes cute becomes annoying, flippant becomes mean, and irritations build up. Mole hills become the proverbial mountains. The pressure of unhappy feelings builds up and erupts.

To avoid that common scenario, we learned the skill of acting on the pinch. When either of us feels violated or hurt, we stop the action, identify the hurt, and explore the partner's intent. Often, the remark is just thoughtless. And, sometimes, hurt comes from the receiver's filters. Usually, we get to do over the action and clear the air.

How do you know when you have a pinch?

How do you sense that your partner feels a pinch?

How can the two of you stop the action and do over?

Share with each other *knee to knee.*

Getting a Word in Edgewise

We watched the Nuthatch creep headfirst down the tree trunk to feeder level, raise his shoulders, spread his wing feathers to appear twice his size, and clearly inform the hungry Chickadees that it was his turn for sunflower seed.

We were reminded of a husband who learned to give clear messages when he needed time to talk with his wife. He was a thoughtful person. It took some time for him to figure out what he was feeling and what he wanted to say. Whenever he got ready to share his heart with his wife, their lovely children flew into the middle; they needed Mama First and Now—and the moment was gone. He could not get a word in edgewise. Like the Nuthatch, he had to learn to clearly speak for his intent: "Hey Gal. I love you. I know now is not possible, but I need some time to connect with you alone." His wife learned to recognize his clearer signals, to honor his intent, and respond by making time or setting time for the two of them to be alone and talk. They both had to leave less to guesswork. They could love their children and each other well.

To protect and nurture a marriage, both individuals must learn to send clear messages about their wish to stay in touch with each other. Both people must learn to be alert for each other's signals and to listen with their hearts.

Consider these questions. Take time to turn to your mate and share your responses *knee to knee.*

What are our signals to each other that say "I love you, and I need some time to be with you, to talk with you?"

How could you make your signals more clear?

How do you wish to have your signals acknowledged?

Spring

A Hair in My Soup

Angry feelings that we are not allowed to voice in our daily work worlds, or which we don't admit to having, are often vented on our partners. We hurt the ones we love most. We have always had dogs and cats. Animal hair is part of our daily environment. Approaching a bowl of chicken and dumplings, Sylvia's equivalent of liquid love, Eddie sarcastically snarled, "There's a hair in my soup," whereupon, Sylvia dissolved into sobs. After two hours of damage control, Eddie said, "It wasn't about you; it was about my graduate prelim committee. I'm stressed and I'm angry."

From then on, we learned to recognize that kind of outburst by the code name "a hair in my soup." Stopping the action and identifying the outburst as such allows us to more quickly move on to the real issue and prevent further hurt.

Do you have code words that help give you safe conduct as a couple through life's minefields?

Can you create, or watch for opportunities to create, some code words?

Share *knee to knee.*

The Tax Man Cometh

Have you ever avoided an issue or a task and found a blessing when you finally faced it together? Or, if you know the old story, have you ever moved a manure pile and actually found a pony underneath? Have you ever put off filing your taxes? Last year, we delayed to the last minute, assuming we were going to have to pay in, and we didn't.

People avoid facing unknowns. We may get frightened and avoid even naming the issues out loud, yet it is likely that our partners have similar fears. We put off redoing our wills, and we avoided looking at the details of our long term financial plans because we feared asking tough questions. When, with encouragement, we began to break the tasks into steps we could complete, we were able to face our dreads together and were strengthened as a couple. Life is not all "a bed of roses," but we are much relieved to be moving forward together.

Have you faced some looming issue and come out stronger?

Do you as individuals or as a couple have any looming issues that need naming?

What could you do to get started?

Share together *knee to knee.*

A Couple's Day Out

Why not take a couple's day out? Small towns or neighborhoods in cities hold possibilities for refreshing getaways from daily responsibilities and make chances for married people to reconnect with their spouses. They are the kind of time all couples need. But, to happen, they have to be planned.

One spring, we spent a day in a nearby small town. We parked at our favorite used book store, walked our hour, looped the town, explored old homes and admired the Bleeding Hearts in full bloom at the Veteran's Memorial; we greeted other walkers, stopped to mail a letter, and found the old elementary school. Backtracking by the retired grain elevator Garden Center, we bought a flat of impatiens. Relaxing over coffee and scones gave us a second wind to rummage in the book store to replenish the summer supply. It was not a day for serious conversation. It was a day for holding hands, "Look at that," and "I'm glad to be with you!"

What ideas do you have for a couple's day out?

Share your ideas with your spouse *knee to knee.*

Get busy and plan a Couple's Day Out.

Setting Goals

Seeking some flatland hiking one spring, we ventured to Cumberland, a Georgia barrier island. In the backcountry on the inland side, we sought a tent site. We chose a spot far back from the shore and higher than the tidal debris line. At 3:30 AM, we were awakened by bubbling that, for the entire world, sounded like an old coffee percolator commercial. Shining the light outside, we considered whether a raccoon could lap water that loudly. Moments later, we realized that our tent was floating up around us on its waterproof floor. The tide had come up through the fiddler crab burrows in the ground beneath us. Pulling stakes, we carried the tent to higher ground.

Have you ever set your goals too low? We sought the comfort of level ground and discovered that it did not guarantee even a dry night's sleep. Setting goals can keep us mindful of moving our marriage in a positive direction.

Have you set your goals for your marriage at comfort level?

What would constitute higher ground?

What goals are important to each of you?

Set some short term and some longer term goals for your marriage? Write them down.

What will each of you contribute toward reaching those goals?

Be specific. Set a time to evaluate your progress.

Consider these questions individually and with your mate *knee to knee.*

Leftovers

Eddie is an avid gardener. He and his tiller unearth countless artifacts from the previous life of the garden plot. Horseshoes, glass, arrowheads, and an engine manifold are recent treasures. In our marriages, we encounter leftovers from our former lives that do not belong to us as a couple. They may relate to family of origin issues, otherwise known as FOOI (phooey). They may come from earlier relationships, old hurts, mistrust, and guardedness.

When leftovers are triggered with our partners, we can identify them because they come with more heat, fire, and noise than what is called for by the current circumstances. At our house, when the heat surprises us, it is a cue to stop, look, and listen. One of us will calmly ask, “Where in the world did that come from?” We both understand that coded question acknowledges that the heat might not be all about our partner. Together, we then try to figure out the source of the high emotion. The acknowledgement makes the situation safer for us as a couple and allows us to behave more gently with each other.

Are you vulnerable in specific areas?

Do you know where those vulnerabilities come from?

Where is your spouse vulnerable?

Can you learn to say to one another "that was not about you"?

Share *knee to knee.*

Quiet

Quiet is a rare commodity. In our busyness, we hardly know what to do with quiet when it happens to us. Recognizing it and naming it are the first steps to enjoying it together.

Quiet often comes by surprise and holds a sense of wonder. It may arrive when the children are in bed or with the grandparents, or when we find ourselves together watching the children play, or early in the morning, or late at night, or when everything else is still enough that we can hear the breeze in the trees or the birds singing. We can almost hear each other's heart beating. Our job is to stop and identify the quiet to our mate. We can then just be in the moment, breathe it in, and savor it together.

When were some times when you and your partner shared quiet?

Share some treasures *knee to knee.*

Make a pledge to identify quiet to your mate the next time you sense it so you can enjoy it together.

The Sounds of Your Love

Listening to the "oldies" station in the car together, we burst out with words from long term memory. Relationships are multi-sensory. People may like different brands of music, but there is music surrounding almost everything we do. Lyrics stick with us when they touch something we are experiencing. They can make us laugh or cry. The songs we share are part of our bond with each other. We courted to some, spending time in the car together and dancing most college nights in the student center. We honeymooned to some and learned others from friends. Music captures life. Sharing the memories evoked grows our marital bond.

Other sounds may be part of the experiences of a marriage: backyard laughter, babies "crashing" in the grocery store line, someone's accent, even the sound of footsteps on the porch and the door opening that says, "He's home."

What are the sounds of your love?

What sounds makes you smile together?

Talk it over with your spouse *knee to knee.*

Prepare for Change

"Lane Closures Ahead." "New Stop Lights at Exit 24." Warning signs on highways tell us to plan ahead in order to take appropriate action. Couples need to focus on things that are coming up and make time to discuss them together. Change in life is a given. Many changes are predictable. New babies change the couple. Jobs demand change. Parenting teens, caring for aging parents, having an empty nest, retiring—all are somewhat predictable.

Consider using "If-Then" scenarios. Explore feelings, observe the strategies of other couples, and brainstorm possibilities before action is demanded. These practices can help keep partners intentionally in touch with each other as change approaches.

Consider together *knee to knee.*

What changes have you weathered as a couple?

What changes do you predict you will face next?

What can you do to prepare for these changes?

What Makes You Laugh?

What makes you laugh? Life without laughter would be dull and sad. Likewise, marriage should never be all work; marriage needs shared laughter. There is a big difference in laughing at someone and laughing with someone. Laughing at someone hurts; laughing with someone joins the two of you. Our senses of humor are truly individual. It takes time and experience to appreciate each other's senses of humor as sources of richness in our marriage.

In that richness, we see that our shared laughter is triggered by a variety of situations. The antics of our kids or pets, comic strips that reflect our life at some stage, particularly crazy billboards, or some comedies seem like obvious sources. Less obvious is the laughter triggered by incongruity, things that are hilarious because they are true but don't seem to fit together at all, like the things our mothers said in dementia, or the things we said in anger, *after* we realized how ridiculous we sounded. Laughter provides much needed release from stress as it exercises our muscles and pops our endorphins. Laughing together grows our marriage muscles.

What do you appreciate about your spouse's sense of humor?

What do you appreciate about laughter in your marriage?

What silly things do you remember from the early days of your relationship?

When has laughter saved the day?

Turn to your spouse and share *knee to knee.*

Guarding the Cooler

Leaving the campsite to go to the beach, Ed said, “Don’t let the raccoons see you latch that cooler.” “Yeh, right, sure,” I responded. When we returned to camp, the cooler was open, the campsite was strewn with a dozen empty egg shells, spaghetti strands, an empty margarine tub, and assorted chewed containers. The culprits bolted for the scrub. Who would have thought they could get that latch open? The moral: Never underestimate the intelligence of the "beasts."

The worlds of work and community are very smart "beasts" in the ways they can grab us, our time, talents, commitment and energy, to do their bidding. Surely, the tasks at work must be done, a living must be earned, and community needs must be met, as well, but we must maintain control of our personal “cooler latches.” We must have some choice in our levels of involvement outside of our family. It is easy to be caught in a flattering plea that you are the “only one” who can do a job. However worthy they may be, when too many good causes rob “the cooler,” they limit the energy we have to spend, and our couple and family relationships can suffer.

Consider the following questions with your mate *knee to knee.*

What good causes are raiding your "cooler" and robbing you of time and energy needed at home?

Responsibilities and activities do have beginnings and endings. What choices will you have sometime soon?

How might you guard your "latch" better to have more time and energy for each other and your family?

Destination

Destination occasions on beaches or at resorts are popular for weddings and anniversaries. Why not plan a couple's destination event? The internet makes it easy to find something that suits the two of you perfectly. We planned our Chattanooga escape around our college's formal at the Tennessee Aquarium. We arrived early, checked into a classic old hotel, dressed up, and walked to the party. The next morning, we enjoyed a leisurely breakfast, walked in the Bluffs Art District along the river, and played Frisbee in the park. We headed home refreshed.

What destinations tempt you?

Are there closer, more doable possibilities? We don't always need to wait for big blocks of time and money to become available.

Talk about what you and your mate would like to do *knee to knee.*

Planning for Heavy Loads

Once, we decided that it was easier to haul a log splitter downhill to the cabin than to haul the logs uphill to the splitter. WRONG!!! It was all good until we attempted to pull the splitter back uphill. With tires spinning, the vehicle refused to go. We tried again with a longer tow. Bad idea! One yelled "NO;" the other heard "GO." So similar –"GO," "WHOA," and "NO." It is a wonder we survived. Couples need to plan ahead before attempting to handle heavy loads.

Both physical and emotional loads can be heavy. Misunderstandings are predictable. When it occurs to even one of us that a load might be **heavy**, we need to slow down, pay attention, and ask ourselves and each other some questions:

Is this load heavy?
What needs to be done here?
How could we get into trouble in this situation?
What result do we want here?
What plan could we make and both try to follow?

Talk this situation over with your partner *knee to knee.*

What loads are physically or emotionally heavy for you?

Do you wish you had handled past heavy loads in different ways?

Make a couple code word for safer handling of heavy loads in the future.

Beans and Franks

When Faith and Joe were first married, they had no money, but they had each other, their love, and shared hope for the future. On their first wedding anniversary, the larder contained a lonely can of beans and franks. For the next 50+ years, laughter with beans and franks marked the occasion of their anniversary.

What everyday things have been transformed into symbols of your love because you experienced them together?

Of what do they remind you?

Are they part of your rituals?

Share your thoughts *knee to knee.*

Summer

Boblo Boat

The City Mouse took the Country Mouse on a walk on the Detroit riverfront—not a place he would have approached with comfort. Going there at all was a gift of love. Out of the blue, he showed more flexibility than she expected by offering a river cruise. She was shocked and thrilled. Moving downriver, they passed the old Boblo Island Amusement Park excursion boat just returned from Toledo for restoration. The boat was a shell but the blown glass stairwell windows were intact. She spontaneously shared all the delight of making the trip with friends as a young teen, feeling terribly grown up. It was a tale untold for 40 years.

What delighted you when you were a young teen?

Share with each other *knee to knee.*

Did you learn something new about each other?

"Used" Produce and Other Surprises

We head directly for the "clearance" section of the produce department when we go shopping. We have found an unexpected source of adventure—the "just right" mango or papaya, bananas we don't need to wait to ripen, baby artichokes cheap enough to buy, fennel bulb, and celery root. Some items are things we have never tried before. Perhaps we have read about them or seen them on television. Culinary adventures are waiting for us if we open our eyes.

Marital adventures are, too! How about visiting a church on vacation? Finding a new place to walk? Scheduling a marriage enrichment cruise? Opening the newspaper weekly entertainment guide and picking one wild and crazy or maybe just brand new thing to do or place to visit together? Like the exotic produce we have incorporated into our meals, you may find new ways to experience and enjoy each other.

MAKE TIME to find an adventure with your mate!

Talk over your craziest ideas *knee to knee*. Brainstorm—listen.

OR JUST GO and see what happens.

Falling Off the Wagon

Sometimes, despite all of our good intentions, we fall off the wagon in our marriages. We determine how we want to act, to treat our partners lovingly, to really listen, and then….something happens. Our old defensiveness rears up, and we blow it. Rather than give in and give up, we have the choice to choose to say, "I'm sorry. That is not what I wish I had said. Please, let me try that over again."

In the very next second, we can acknowledge our part, make a repair attempt with our partner, and climb back on the wagon of intentional behavior. Make sure your partner knows you are attempting a repair.

What does it feel like to "blow it?"

How do you reconnect with your mate?

How does your partner reach out to reconnect with you?

Talk this over *knee to knee*, and pledge to climb back on the wagon the very next second.

To Do or To Be?

During an obligatory exercise walk in a new town, we tripped over the Amtrak station. Curiously, we perused the schedule; “Oh, it goes to Chicago!” On a whim, we got tickets to go to Chicago for lunch, six hours one way. At 6:45 AM the next morning, we boarded with books to read and articles to write. At midnight, we returned home, never having opened the pack. With the rhythm of the train, the conversations about the towns we passed, and the coziness of the space, the “to do list” gave way to “to be.” We were amazed at the intimacy of our time together. Next time, we plan to stay overnight and chill a little longer.

When have you experienced letting go of the "to do list?"

What does it feel like to just "be" together?

Cast Upon the Shore

Every couple experiences stormy weather. Walking at dusk on Jekyll Island, we stepped around and over countless jellyfish cast up by the storm and stranded by the receding tide. They were a mess left to feed the gulls. We have felt like those jelly fish looked. We have had some years that were full of health and job crises for ourselves and for those we love. Even with loving support and prayers, communication skills, and excellent care in those times, we felt wrecked, tossed, and out of control. Unlike those jellyfish, our plight was temporary. We can reclaim our anchor points, make our plans together, right our ship and move on.

When did you feel like the jellyfish?

How did you right your ship?

What have you learned about yourself and your partner?

What helped you when the next storm arrived?

Share *knee to knee*

Honoring the Kid Inside

When we crammed two separate high school reunions into one year, it was not convenient. They were out of state two weeks apart. We both wanted to go, and we both wanted to go together. At my reunion, someone cracked, "Ed must be making payback for you going to his reunion." No way—we wanted to share with each other the personal space that helped to shape the kids we still carry around inside of us.

While I knew Eddie's home town well, he had only dropped into mine for quick visits during college summers when we were courting, and my family had later moved away. As we wandered through the high school halls and walked "home from school" and back that day, I felt like he better understood the part of me who had grown up, played, studied, birthday partied, taken dance, swimming and driving lessons, and first loved, in that place.

When Eddie was eight years old, his dad bought a greenhouse which he ran for extra income. Gardens have always been part of what we do, but, when Eddie got his own greenhouse, "the dirtiest little boy in Grayling" was reborn. As I watch him from the house, moving inside the greenhouse, planting, flatting, tending his babies, gifting friends, I see him as he is now and as he was. My heart is touched to hear him say, "These are the best tomato plants I have ever grown; my dad would be proud."

How do you see the child inside of your spouse?

What do you appreciate about the child in him or her?

Honor your spouse with your thoughts *knee to knee*.

Being Marriage Friendly

Weddings are events in which family, friends, and co-workers join with couples to celebrate the beginning of a new time in the cycle of life. Parties are planned, gifts are given, special wardrobes are purchased, prayers are said, and promises are made. Most people wish the couple many blessings in their lives as husbands and wives, but, then, people largely walk away and leave couples alone to figure out how to be and stay married. As wonderful as marriage can be, it is never easy. Men and women who are experiencing great happiness find few listeners either. If they are happy, they are expected to keep it to themselves.

Couples need other people, including other couples, who value marriage and who can build them up in rough times and rejoice with them in good times. They seldom find someone who offers to hold them in prayer and encourage them. Marriages need marriage friendly contexts.

How can you be part of the marriage friendly context for other couples?

Whose marriages do you hold sacred?

Whose marriages do you wish well?

Whose marriages do you uphold?

Have you told them? You are needed.

Share your thoughts with your spouse *knee to knee.*

Spontaneity

Have you and your mate been spontaneous this week? Lately? Maybe you can remember; maybe you have to think about it. Spontaneity can be fun; spontaneity can help us grow.

We went to Florida for a *Better Marriages* getaway. After a particularly harried race to make our flight because I left my purse in Security, I impulsed a rental upgrade to a Sebring convertible. It was a gorgeous day. We basked in the sunshine. Ed complained mightily that I couldn't put him in a hot car and then bug him about speeding. He even flashed back to a rental Mustang in Washington, D.C. in summer 1970 and had to take my picture with this car, too. We cruised up the coast in style.

The next day, Ed insisted we grab a sandwich and picnic at the beach in the car, right before leading our workshop. I agreed, having to calm my controlling self. And, Ed was right-- again. When we arrived at our workshop, on time and giggling, half our couples were carrying box lunches because the hotel restaurant had been so slow. I had been with a great guy in a "hot" car, sticky with chocolate cake, relishing a sea breeze, while I could have been insisting we must lunch at the hotel. We were a little goofy, but I will remember that day with a smile and remind myself that spontaneity is a good thing.

Think of a spontaneous time together that makes you smile.

Share that experience and celebrate with each other *knee to knee.*

Where were you?

What happened?

How did you feel?

Why do you like that memory?

Making Memories

We have laughed at the advertisement squirrels marking the hiding places for their nuts with "sticky notes." It occurs to us that we humans all have individual memories, but to share those memories with our partner takes extra care. When do we know that an experience is such a treasure that we want to keep it forever? It can begin with an emotion that makes us pay closer attention to the details.

Watching our new granddaughter awake with a spontaneous smile for Grandma, I saw Sylvia's tears and felt my own. It was a moment I could touch. I knew we were standing on holy ground. Acknowledging the emotion and identifying the specialness of that moment to my wife made it part of the cement that holds us together. We can revisit that moment anytime we remind each other about it. We love Abby; we love each other.

Treasuring common memories brings couples closer together. Memories include times of happiness, contentment, excitement, nearness, pride and, sometimes, sadness. They remind us that we have shared wonderful experiences. They remind us that we have weathered storms and survived. They help us to count our blessings out loud.

Be on the lookout for special moments in your daily activities. Share your awareness with your partner. Put names, or mental "sticky notes," on them so you can help each other recall them later.

Describe to your partner a moment you could touch that you want to revisit.

Name it so you can treasure and cherish it as part of your life together.

Share some of your memories of your life together *knee to knee.*

Regular Scheduled Maintenance

Our home needs regular scheduled maintenance: the siding around the outside faucet is crumbling; the privet is overgrowing the fence; a heat pump is over 20 years old. Cars need oil changes, hoses, transmissions flushed. Our bodies fare a little better; we see some doctor every three months, pacemaker checks, blood work. Extended family relationships need nurturing. Jobs require continuing education and licensures; we can't let those requirements lapse, can we?

Likewise, our marriages need regular scheduled maintenance. We say "I do," and somehow expect our marriages to keep up with us as we fly through our two lives. Demands pull us away from each other and the joy we can experience as married partners in life. When we married, we made some promises to each other before God and in the presence of our community. Churches, agencies, and marriage enrichment groups offer many opportunities for marital growth.

Will you think about your vows and commit to cherish your spouse in some program this fall? Time conflicts come immediately to mind; we all have them. Will you be like one young husband? He and his wife wanted to do a program for their marriage, and they had a busy family schedule. He gave his wife a wonderful gift. He responded to her worry, "It's important; *we'll* make it happen." And they did.

Explore making a commitment to your marriage in a couples' program this year *knee to knee.*

What opportunities are available?

What would you like to do?

Who will take the next step of registering?

Attitude Adjustment

When I hear the word 'attitude,' I hear it in an accusing tone. In fact, I have used it many times in an accusing tone, as in "It's your attitude," or "You need an attitude adjustment." Even if it occurs to me to say the words to myself, I want to duck, because it usually means I am going to have to make a change. Likely, I am going to have to give up controlling something that I prefer to control.

Control can get work done, and it gives a temporary illusion of safety. It can, also, make misery for the controller and the controlled, especially in marriage. With control, one needs to ask, "Is my behavior getting me where I want to go?" "Is it getting in the way of feeling good about marriage and my mate?"

Attitude adjustment can take the form of reframing—a much more friendly word. Power outages are common at our cabin. We can't control when the grid will be restored, but we can consciously choose our attitude. Every bucket of water brought from the lake for flushing is a gift for or from our mate. And, we have a lake full of water! Situations may be annoying or difficult, but we do not need to make each other miserable. Reframing is a choice to see ourselves and our mates differently.

If control behavior is familiar—own your own first. Remember that your mate doesn't like being confronted any more than you do.

Talk with each other *knee to knee* about situations you could reframe so your feelings and the atmosphere in your marriage could be improved.

Needing Support

Getting up before dawn, not for our walk, but for a run to the hospital for fasting blood tests can be a lonely time. It seems that tasks related to health can make people feel particularly vulnerable and lonely. Ed's offer to just ride along and keep me company was welcome and has grown into something we do for each other whenever possible.

We were taught to be independent individuals; however, we have found that we were not so well taught about when it is okay to ask for support. There are many things in life we must do alone, but sometimes it is just nice to have a buddy.

Coming out of our selves and being aware of when the other might need support is an art that couples develop over time. We need to become creative in the ways we give support. We also need to learn to ask our partner for support and be clear about what we need. Most of us don't want to be told what to do, nor do we want to have our feelings minimized or seen as silly. Listening and keeping company can help to make things just a little better. That may be all we need or all we can do.

When do you feel the need for quiet support from your spouse?

How would you like your spouse to respond?

When might your spouse need that kind of support?

How do you respond to your spouse?

Share your thoughts on these questions with your spouse *knee to knee*.

In Sickness and In Health

When we took our wedding vows, we promised to take each other "to have and to hold...in sickness and in health." We surely did not dwell on the sickness phrase, yet, if couples are fortunate enough to live together for a long time, we are called to live out that vow. Sickness is difficult for both partners. When Ed fell and broke his hip, we learned again that sickness breeds scary feelings like fragility, helplessness, inadequacy, and fear of abandonment. Role definitions are scrambled. Tasks always done jointly must be done singly. Fear of loss of capability threatens both partners.

When the immediate crisis passes, there is a natural drop in the stress hormones that help us get through the pain and shock. In the letdown, being patient with healing is another challenge. Finally, we can take some time to verbally and physically comfort each other, to share our individual experiences and fears, and to appreciate how love and faith have brought us through once more.

In your marriage, have there been difficult times of sickness or injury?

How have you handled them as a couple?

What helped you to survive?

Look back and affirm your partner *knee to knee.*

Fall

Music in your Marriage

We have always been conscious of music in our relationship. We danced to the jukebox in the Union at Alma College; we still dance whenever we get the opportunity. So what is music in marriage? Some songs speak to us through the years.

Musical elements can be related to marriage. Melody in marriage equals regular day to day life--daily sharing times, planning meals, making a home. Harmony equals communication, new learning, shared experiences, and conflicts resolved. Percussion equals heat and anger, as well as play, laughter, and excitement. Mood Music equals sexuality. Grace notes equal surprises.

All the elements are important, but don't forget rhythm. That back beat is commitment, a constant heartbeat underneath that keeps us going for the long term. We can turn up the volume on our commitment.

Do you remember music from your courtship?

What is the back beat of your marriage?

What could you do as individuals and as a couple to grow commitment in your relationship?

Talk it over with your partner *knee to knee.*

Who Is Speaking Now?

On our campus, there is a carillon tower which serves as the college clock. Bells of different sizes with different tones play hymns and chime the hours as students scamper to class or lunch. In our lives, we play multiple roles, and each role, like a bell, has its own tone of voice. The tone matches the tasks and relationships of the roles. We are sons or daughters, fathers or mothers, bread winners, teachers, bosses, employees. Our roles as husbands and wives are closer to those of friends, colleagues, or team members. When one of us uses a tone that does not fit our marriage relationship, someone objects: "I am not your child." "I am not one of your students."

We are learning to be aware of the tone of voice we are using with each other. Does it match the kind of husband or wife we want to be with each other? Sometimes, it is difficult to switch from parent or manager to partner. We are learning to say, "Wait. I just heard the tone of my voice. It had to do with something that happened today. What I would like for you to hear is different. Can I try it over again?"

Do you use tones that belong with other roles when speaking to your partner?

Can you better monitor your tone?

Is it hard to switch from your work roles to your home roles?

Are entry points at the end of the day difficult?

How could you and your partner work together to connect at the end of the day in ways that affirm your relationship?

Share your thoughts with each other *knee to knee.*

Abundance

How do we reject the mentality of scarcity that permeates our marriages? There is never enough time or money to adequately honor our partners, so we spend much of our lives waiting and longing. We say, "Later, Honey, Too busy." Or we think, "After we get caught up, we'll get away."

Our marriage can't wait for the getaway. We must look at what we do have. In our shed, an ounce of ant killer left in the sack is useless; an open bag of fertilizer turns to concrete; partial cans of paint take up space. They are wasted. Compliments not given and thank yous left unsaid are lost opportunities, as well.

When we adopt a mentality of abundance, we CAN find five minutes to sit side by side and cuddle or talk quietly. We CAN give a hot dog supper some style with a split of domestic champagne by candlelight. We CAN give words of praise without any discussion allowed.

Affirm your partner NOW. Waste not; want not.

Enjoy together, *knee to knee.*

Oops

On the job, Ed's dad parked his truck, enjoyed his cheese sandwich, and took a snooze. Refreshed, he proceeded to back up—WHAM—an 8 inch spruce seemed to have grown up behind the back bumper during his lunch break. Likewise, the witch across the street from us has whammed into the telephone pole AGAIN and looks very surprised.

When we encounter the unexpected, we have a crisis. We usually get through the crisis, but, sometimes, we could do a better job of coming through together if we were more practiced in using our best communication skills.

What unanticipated trees, telephone poles, or other obstacles has your marriage encountered?

How did you handle the crisis as individuals and as a couple?

What skills helped you to survive?

What skills do you need to practice? They are your portable tool kit.

Talk it over with your mate *knee to knee.*

Money, Money, Money

At *Better Marriages* gatherings, we choose some workshops that will allow us to play and some that we know will make us stretch. At Unicoi State Park, in our early forties, we decided to stretch in a workshop on financial planning--money.

After the workshop, Ed wanted to buy a gift for me, a beautiful quilt that reminded him of his grandmother. Wanting to honor his wish to give a gift, but uneasy, I offered, “What if we were to spend the same money on a financial plan?” In the next months, with the help of a marriage enrichment friend who was a financial planner, we were freed of much of the fear associated with money and the future. We reframed how we saved and invested to match our time of life and family’s needs. We lost the defensive guilt that came from being afraid we had been bad managers. We learned to talk about money and plan rather than to avoid talking about it and to be afraid. What a blessing!

How do you feel about money at the present time?

What will your needs be in the future?

Could talking with a financial planner be useful?

Talk it over with your partner *knee to knee.*

Holidaze Eminent

As we exchanged the summer wreath on the front porch for the Halloween wreath, ghosts, and fall leaf garland, it occurred to us that the Holidaze is eminent. We are quickly headed into the most holiday packed part of the year. It is a time filled with activities and emotions. We each have expectations, and others have expectations of us. There will be a whirlwind of activities from Thanksgiving travel to Christmas parties for every group where we belong.

We each carry memories of the past and hopes for this season. Some memories will come from our childhoods; some have been made with our mates. We each have our own personal reactions to the approach of the holidays. Right now is not too early to take an intentional hold on the season. If we don't start now, the season will be in charge, and we will get what it brings.

As a couple, use the following questions to get your thoughts and feelings to surface:

Are there things you do to prepare for this time of year, for the holidays?

How do you feel about gifts—choosing, giving, receiving?

What emotions do you associate with the season? Are all feelings positive, or are they mixed? Are there losses associated with the season?

What are your favorite parts of the season? --your least favorite parts?

Can you, or, do you want to make changes in how you and your family celebrate this year? If so, what might they be?

Share your thoughts with your mate *knee to knee.*

Together, make plans to approach, survive, and enjoy the season in ways that are meaningful for both of you.

Appreciation: A Little Grease

Seeing his recoil from the butter dish, Ed's Aunt Bertha, who never ever had a weight problem in spite of owning a Dairy Bar, reminded her newly "at goal" Weight Watcher nephew that her doctor told her everyone needs a little grease for the joints. In our marriage, we would call that "healthy oil." Daily busyness distracts us from focusing on our partner. Marriages need sweet romantic gestures and expressions of appreciation to "keep the joints moving."

Ed brings flowers from the garden, or from a field trip, or from the greenhouse. I know that every flower says, "I love you." He thinks an unrequested cup of coffee and any meal that takes more than one step is extra special. I know that accepting his invitation to join him in the hammock, even for a few minutes, makes us both feel calmer and closer. It makes deposits in our love bank, lowers frustration, and makes us better able to face the normal demands of our lives.

How do you show appreciation for your partner?

How does your partner provide peace in the storm for you?

What actions or words "grease" the joints of your life together?

Thank each other *knee to knee.*

Where Are You Headed?

The "front" and the "back" of a rail car are determined by the position of the engine. Half of the seats face each direction. If you want to travel facing forward (toward the destination), you have to know where the engine is coupled. If you can't see the engine, you rely on your body's senses to tell you how the train is moving. Are you moving forward or backward?

In our marriages, we need to determine how to face forward and not revisit the Baggage Car where some of our less successful ways of interacting may be riding.

What do your senses tell you about the direction your marriage is traveling?

Does the direction match your intended destination for your marriage?

Do you need to "change seats" in any way to face in the direction you wish to travel?

Talk it over *knee to knee.*

Remembering to say "Thank You"

It is that time of year when colors change, fall wreaths appear beside doors, piles of pumpkins lean on fence posts, and people take a few days to concentrate on counting their blessings before the Christmas rush takes over. Putting mind, and heart, over matter is a challenge in the busyness of life; however, saying "Thank You" is essential to marriage.

I am grateful for a life partner who knows my history and my dreams for the future.
I am grateful for a husband who knows my inner thoughts most of the time, but takes time to listen to hear if I have changed my mind or come up with a new insight.
I am grateful for a husband who loves the Lord and the church and is not afraid to act out of that love.
I am grateful for a husband with whom to share children and grandchildren as we parent through a lifetime.
I am grateful for a husband who takes new adventures with me even when he is not entirely comfortable with them.
I am grateful for a husband who feels so familiar to me that I take comfort in his physical presence.

Take time to say "Thank You" to your mate, *knee to knee.* It is important for us as individuals and in our marriages.

Get Strong in the Basics

Periodic dance lessons are one way that we play. Dancing is a skill. It takes intentionality and practice just like communicating with each other. When we watch professional dancers, it all looks so smooth, nimble, and effortless. A closer look shows sweat. Our teacher preached, "Get strong in the basics." The basics can make dance graceful and fun even before you add the flourishes.

A basic for our marriage is to concentrate on speaking for ourselves as individuals and listening to our partner. Listening and mirroring what we think the other person is saying, before assuming we understand, shows we honor each other even if we disagree. That behavior emphasizes the friendship part of our relationship. Our friendship is more important than any immediate issue.

How are you doing on the basics?

What do you personally need to remember?

Speak for your own use of communication skills, and talk it over *knee to knee.*

Find some Mistletoe

All kinds of magazines are prescribing kissing as a way to wake up and energize a marriage. Try adding a one minute kiss to your daily routine. Count the seconds. It may make you come up for air; it may make you laugh. We couldn't make it for a full ten seconds without a breath in the Wyoming mountains.

Enjoyment of your husband or wife is a gift intended by God for your pleasure and for reaffirming your bond no matter how long you have been married. At this time of year, you even have the excuse of mistletoe hanging in doorways, hallways, and porches. Maybe you can kiss more than once a day.

Where was your first kiss?

Are there other memorable kisses?

Make one.

Celebrate to Activate

We set goals and make Marriage Growth Plans. When we renew our plans, some items seem to move on to the next year and to the next without our making noticeable progress. Such issues were health, weight loss, and exercise. We would beat ourselves up and then do nothing else. Guilt got us nowhere.

Light bulbs flashed when we instead chose to celebrate what we had accomplished. We had prioritized couple time. We had moved forward with financial planning. In the mood of celebration, we found new energy to take baby steps into the dreaded health issues. With some positive results, we activated more energy to reenroll in dance lessons adding fun and romance to exercise!

Where have you made progress toward goals? No fair saying "nowhere."

Brainstorm fun ways to celebrate what you have accomplished.

What is your next step?

Marriage Growth Plan

It is time for a Marriage Growth Plan for next year.

Individually list; then combine lists:

Three things you want for yourself

Three things you want for your mate

Three things you want for your marriage

Now, make a plan together *knee to knee.*

Include goals for:

short term (two week)

mid term (6 month)

long term (a year or more)

Include steps for each goal, and responsibilities for the steps.

Make dates to evaluate along the way. Put them on your calendars.

____

____

Sign, date, and seal with a kiss.

HAPPY NEW YEAR!!

Resources

www.eddieandsylviarobertson.com

www.bettermarriages.org

www.bettermarriagesga.org

www.couplecommunication.com

www.fivelovelanguages.com

www.prepare-enrich.com